TAROT KEYWORDS A

Also by Marcia J. Kenyon

The Butterfly Collection, 2013

Shades of Light and Dark, 2014

TAROT KEYWORDS AND MEANINGS

By

Marcia J. Kenyon

For my sons, Craig and Rob Galley.

FOOL

Planet – **Uranus**

Fresh start

Crossroads and decisions

Break free from the past

Avoid foolish behaviour

Personal discovery

New opportunities

Excitement and enthusiasm

Taking intuitive risks

Freedom and innocence

Unconventional sex life

The child within us

Nervous tension and mental energy

Learn from past mistakes

MAGICIAN

Planet – **Mercury**

A successful person

Make your ideas a reality

An unemotional person

Have a sense of control of your life

Nervous exhaustion

Self-love and confidence

Creativity

Capacity to influence others

Goals achieved

Breathing problems

Self-employment

Determination

New opportunities

Someone will point you in the right direction

HIGH PRIESTESS

Planet – **Moon**

Intuition

Mystery

Secrets

Quest for knowledge

Revealing time ahead

Keep intentions to yourself

Have patience

Pay attention to dreams

A clever lady

Remote/detached person

Affected by moon, menstruation

Genital problems or pregnancy

Only confiding in women

EMPRESS

Planet – **Venus**

Creativity

Financial and material comfort

Harmony and peace

Rewards for hard work

Expansion

Beauty

Links with nature/countryside

Pregnancy or birth

New business

Security

Sexual pleasure

Femininity

Growth

Mother figure

Sensuality

EMPEROR

Star sign – **Aries**

Powerful person

Strong, steady and reliable

Authority and dominance

A father figure

Self-confidence

Intelligent and reasonable

Supportive

Unemotional

Could make life difficult if let down

Security

Respect

Serious person

HIEROPHANT

Star sign – **Taurus**

Conventional behaviour

Stick to tried and tested

Interest in religion

Joining of two people, marriage

Learning, teachers and students

Prefers routine and pays attention to detail

Advice, counsellors

Un-extravagant

LOVERS

Star sign – **Gemini**

Choice between two paths – one right, one wrong

Love and romance entering

Harmony at work

Attractions

Being re-united

Commitment

Marriage

Engagement

Temptation and infidelity

CHARIOT

Star sign – **Cancer**

Hard work and effort

Recognition for efforts

Struggles and opposition

Determination

Encouragement

Exam success and victory

Vehicles and travel

Moving house

Harness difficulties

News arriving

Progress and promotion

Selfish behaviour and conflicting desires

Slow down a little

JUSTICE

Star sign – **Libra**

Fairness

Equality

Honesty

Legal affairs that have favourable outcome

Intellect

Power

Lessons in Karma

The right decision

Well-balanced personality

Choices and decisions

Legal documents to sign

People who make laws

Logical negotiation

Learning and education

HERMIT

Star sign – **Virgo**

Quiet contemplation

Shutting oneself away

Learning something new

Beware of your actions

Unconventional teacher/guide

Prudence

Loneliness, fear

To retreat/withdraw

Doom and gloom

Use discretion

Answer lies within

Study and introspection

Be cautious

WHEEL OF FORTUNE

Planet – **Jupiter**

A change of circumstances - better or for worse

New relationships

Good luck and fortune

Keep making changes to prevent stagnation

Movement

New opportunities

Wheels and travel

Success

New cycle in whatever area the card falls

STRENGTH

Star sign – **Leo**

Inner strength

Recovery from illness

Courage

A difficult task to tackle

Triumph and faith

Resolution

Generous person

Reconciliation and forgiveness

Animals and pets

Achievements and exam success

The power of love will conquer all

Sexual desires fulfilled

HANGED MAN

Planet – **Neptune**

Suspension in affairs

Delays

Mental changes

Spiritual outlook

Sacrifice, giving something up

Good from bad

Commitment through sacrifice

Complete and unexpected change

Taking time to think

Not right time to make decisions

Turn things on their head, look at situation from a different angle

DEATH

Star sign – **Scorpio**

Transformation

End of a situation

Mourning the past

Complete change

Loss of something, job etc

Fresh start

Learn from past

Painful and emotional time

Good from bad

TEMPERANCE

Star sign – **Sagittarius**

Balance

Resolution of a problem

Creative satisfaction

Good manager, team worker

Calm, peace and relaxation

Taking things easy

Moderation

Patience

Mutual respect

Understanding

Don't give up

Harmony

Security

Test water, be cautious

DEVIL

Star sign – **Capricorn**

Temptation

Greed and materialism

Trapped by own doing

Power through money, lust, sex

Emotional blackmail

Excessive behaviour

Indulgence

Selfishness

Oppression

Slavery and victimisation

Sexual abuse

A warning

Be more practical

TOWER

Planet – **Mars**

A shock

Revelations

False structures knocked down

Accident or health problem

Arguments

Disruption, sudden change

Lack of care

Loss

Fresh start forced upon us

Trust destroyed, disgrace

Breakdown of a situation

Anger, short fuse

Good from bad

STAR

Star sign – **Aquarius**

Hope

Good health and relationships

Dream come true

Accomplishment

Inspiration

Positivity and faith

Creativity

Back to nature

Green issues, helping others

Fate and happiness

Promotion, success, exams, learning and education

Expanding horizons, travel

Renewal of sexual feelings

New age/spiritual interests

MOON

Star sign – **Pisces**

Uncertainty

Not a time to make decisions

Deception

Communication problems

Confusion

Bad dreams

Illusion

Trickery and lies

Occult powers

Use intuition

Relationships not close

Sexual inhibitions

Menstruation, contraception problems

Don't be too dependent on others

Creativity

SUN

Planet – **Sun**

Happiness and enjoyment

Invitations

Warm friendships

Confidence

Good health

Achievement and success

Hot countries, summer, holidays

Children important, births etc

Renewed health

Brilliance

Contented relationships

JUDGEMENT

Planet – **Pluto**

An ending

Evaluate the past

Rewards for past efforts

Rejuvenation

Breaking free from past ties

Legal affairs – positive outcome

Renewed energy

Assess relationships

Decisions urgently required

Time to move on

Cards that fall after Judgement will shed light on an issue

THE WORLD

Planet – **Saturn**

Achievement and success

End of a cycle in life

Completion and accomplishment

Projects ending

Creative study

Assertiveness

Family life after being single

Fame and public recognition

An emotional, testing time is over

Journeys and travel

Sexual and emotional fulfilment

Spiritual enlightenment

New beginnings and horizons

THE SUIT OF WANDS REPRESENTS:

Mental/physical energy

Negotiations

Communication

News

Business world

Partnerships

Struggles/challenges

Overdoing work

Travel and movement

Creativity in words

Property

Lively social events

ACE OF WANDS

Development of ideas

Career opportunities

New directions in working life

Creative pursuits

Communication - Business letters, phone calls etc

A birth

Energetic sex life

Taking initiative

Good news and invitations

Negotiations and contracts

A busy and exciting time ahead

TWO OF WANDS

Taking action

The unknown

Moving house, signing contracts

Have courage to succeed

Partnerships, mainly business

Important letter or transaction

Wondering whether to get too involved in a relationship

A highly proud man

Rewarding friendship at work

Taking a bold step

A powerful businessman

THREE OF WANDS

Creative/business success

New opportunities connected with previous projects/friendships

Advice and practical help

Job offers

Business expansion

Travel through work

Good news via letter/telephone

Development of a relationship

Seeking further progress

FOUR OF WANDS

Hard work being rewarded

A break, rest, holiday, peace

Honeymoons and second honeymoons

Satisfaction and enjoyment

Security

Putting down roots

Buying property

Theatre, music, dance, entertainment

Faith

Using intuition

FIVE OF WANDS

Adrenalin

Opposition

Arguments and strife

Travel delays

Fiery competition

Needing clarity

Teasing

Irritation and annoyance

Power struggles

Clashing of ideas

Conflict

Obstacles caused by others

SIX OF WANDS

Winning a fight

Successful negotiations

Right action taken

Well-deserved promotion

Legal triumphs and good news

Tact and patience pays off

Engagement or marriage

Qualifications

Public acclaim

SEVEN OF WANDS

Stiff competition

Rivalry

Courage

A problem to overcome

Challenge in love life

Determination

Under pressure at work

Stand up for yourself

Don't give up

Fight for your rights

EIGHT OF WANDS

A busy period

News, letters and communication

Travel linked to career or study

Expansion

Active social life

New horizons

The outdoors

Acceleration and movement

Swift developments in love

Impulsive sexual encounters

New friends

Freedom

Sports

NINE OF WANDS

Stifled

Hang on to what you've got

You have the strength

At end of tether

Heartbreak and disappointment in love

Hold on to your beliefs

Recovery from illness

One last challenge

Insecurities and uncertainties

Can't go any further

TEN OF WANDS

Burdens and responsibilities

Ambitious pressures

Putting a lot of energy into work

Aiming towards a goal

Overwork, workaholic, stress

Danger in overdoing it

Excessive emotional demands

To be lumbered in some way

Taking on too much

PAGE OF WANDS

Beginning of a creative phase

Journey

Visitors

Messages, news and letters

Beginning of property matters

Lively person full of energy

New relationships

PRINCE OF WANDS

Star sign – **Sagittarius**

Intelligent person

Flighty person

A charmer

Movement and activity

A person who is always on the move

News and invitations

New business ideas put forward

Move of house

Full of good ideas but not putting them into practice

Travel

QUEEN OF WANDS

Star sign – **Leo**

Creative development

Likes being in the limelight

A charming woman

Reliable and affectionate, loyal

Good businesswoman

Full of good ideas and advice

Positive thinker

Clever lady

Lacks confidence, needs reassurance

Hates possessive behaviour

Attractive personality

Hospitable friend

Sexually active and passionate

KING OF WANDS

Star sign – **Aries**

A charismatic person

Pushy, dominant, arrogant

Good communicator

Charming person or host

Warm and generous

Good father, husband

Good advisor

Secure businessman

Excellent leadership qualities

Hard worker

An unavailable man

THE SUIT OF SWORDS REPRESENTS:

Trouble and strife

Swift action

Betrayal/gossip/lies

Justice and legal matters

Professional people

Mental stimulation

Rational and logical thought

Public relations and media

Conflict

Medical problems/operations

Upsurge of energy

Delays

Mental changes

ACE OF SWORDS

Mental changes

Fresh ways of thinking

Justice, legal/tax matters

Powerful influences

Karmic forces

Operation or injection

Sex without love

Male domination

Conflict

Far-reaching consequences in the area the card falls

TWO OF SWORDS

Tension

Stalemate

Unsettled peace

Justice

Calm before the storm

Not confronting problems

Cannot move forward

Afraid of change

Unstable relationship

Conflict and arguments brewing

Possible delays

Things remaining as they are

No improvement in affairs

THREE OF SWORDS

Loss or heartache, tears

Card of blood, illness, operations

Letting things go for the best

Understanding that things have been necessary

Separation

Divorce

Eternal triangle

Relationships that exist in the mind

Obsessive lust

Disruption in career

Miscarriage, abortion

FOUR OF SWORDS

Rest and recuperation

Renewal of physical and mental energies

Medical problem sexually

Gathering strength after illness

Peace and quiet

Take a break from circumstances

Take it easy for a while

Withdraw from the world

FIVE OF SWORDS

Failure

Underhand tactics, gossip, lies

Wounded pride

Opportunity to make good from bad

Limitation

Selfishness

Someone may have left abruptly

Loss through theft

Accept situation and don't fight against it

Unfaithfulness and humiliation

An embarrassing situation

Jealousy and spite

SIX OF SWORDS

Travel over water

Mental journey to peace

Release of tension

Change for better after a difficult choice

Leaving worries behind

A holiday

SEVEN OF SWORDS

Restlessness

Boredom, feeling trapped

Theft of ideas

Unintentional betrayal

Be cautious in affairs

Tension

Using people sexually

Tactlessness

Don't use violence to achieve goals

Being underhand and sneaky

Wanting to escape from problems

EIGHT OF SWORDS

Trapped and tied down

Unhappiness but frightened to change

Bondage, even sexual

Temporary restriction

Problems need analysing before decisions can be made

Prison

Can't think straight

NINE OF SWORDS

Oppression

Negative thinking

Difficult time

Fear

Sickness

Recent bereavement

Despair and misery

Anxiety

A complex situation

Pain and sorrow

Bad dreams

Guilt

Scandal and gossip in love life

Mother causing/having problems

TEN OF SWORDS

A stab in the back

Forced change

General unhappiness

Divorce or breakdown of relationship

An issue that upsets whole family

A clean break needed

Treachery

Depression

Collapse of plans

Betrayal, lies, slander

Be careful in whom you confide

Watch what you sign

End of a negative phase

PAGE OF SWORDS

A very organised person

Games and sports

News, contracts, documents

Enjoyable gossip and scandal

Becoming more intellectual

A young person may be causing concern

Defensive person

Delay in plans

Disappointing news

KNIGHT OF SWORDS

Star sign – **Gemini**

Quick thinking

Confident man

Good reasoning powers

New ideas

Public relations and media

Energetic man

Speed and change

Decisions

Surprising information

Stormy relationship

Communication

Strong man who will defend you

QUEEN OF SWORDS

Star sign – **Aquarius**

An intelligent lady

Rational and logical person/good advisor

Quick witted, analytical mind

Lively social life, conversation

Not involved in deep friendships – skims the surface

Loyal and strong

Hates possessiveness, likes equality

Fond of music

Unavailable woman in an affair

Success in creative pursuits

Jealous woman

Lonely woman or divorcee

Professional lady offering help and advice

KING OF SWORDS

Star sign – **Libra**

Professional man – doctor, lawyer, boss etc

Problems to be dealt with

No sense of humour

Tough character

Excellent logical advice

Reliable, clever, rational

Highly principled person

Well educated

Restless mind – requires lots of mental stimulation

Flirty but not emotional

THE SUIT OF CUPS REPRESENTS:

Friendships and relationships

Love entering or leaving

Great emotion – happy or sad

Creativity

Engagement, marriage

Success in creative pursuits

Loyalty yet betrayal

Past memories, nostalgia

Fun, pleasure, enjoyment

Parties, socialising

Emotional choices/changes

ACE OF CUPS

Nurturing of ideas

Love

Productive phase in career

Fruition of ideas and plans

Pregnancy or birth

Gifts of love

Creativity

Inspiration

Engagement, marriage

Good social life

Companionship

A new start of beneficial nature

Happiness and contentment

TWO OF CUPS

A loving union

Deep understanding of one another

Someone special on the horizon

Happy partnerships/relationships at home and/or work

A joyful event

Commitment

Engagement

Reunion

THREE OF CUPS

Marriage

Pregnancy or birth

Cause for celebration

Success

Good news

Good luck

Gifts and prizes

Fun and laughter

FOUR OF CUPS

Feeling discontented

You must be the one to bring changes

Re-evaluate your life

Boredom and loneliness

Laziness, not making an effort

Unhappy with friends

Mild depression

Take up new interests

Emotionally scarred

Afraid to let go in love

FIVE OF CUPS

Grieving

Betrayal of trust

Broken vows

Disappointment with partner

Healing emotional wounds

One-sided partnership

Something lost, something gained

Deep sorrow and regret

Expectations unreal

Must try harder in the future

SIX OF CUPS

Memories of the past

Past talents re-surfacing

Past efforts rewarded

Past lovers come back

Reconciliation after separation

Need to go back to roots in order to pursue future plans

Family gathering

Nostalgia

Inheritance

SEVEN OF CUPS

Many different choices

Confusing time

Not right time to decide

Sexual desires and fantasies

Illusions and doubt

Wait and see

EIGHT OF CUPS

Letting go of emotional ties

Rejection in search of meaning

Unsettled

A journey of self-discovery

Leaving the past behind

Doubts about leaving

Miserable situation

Reflect on past before letting go

Travel over water

Searching for deeper meaning of life

NINE OF CUPS

Wish card

Dreams come true

Happiness and satisfaction

Emotional/material gain

Good health

Reason to be pleased with yourself

Don't be smug

Very loving phase

Ideas come easily

Everything running smoothly

Self-love

TEN OF CUPS

Lasting happiness

Permanence

Valuable friendships

Pleasurable relationships

Results, success, attainment

Bliss

Absolute commitment

Marriage

An enjoyable journey

Joy

PAGE OF CUPS

News of a birth

A good idea

New project

Studying

Considerate partner

Gentle person

Development of new feelings

Increased awareness of emotion

Happy, emotional news

Sensitive lover

A creative and clever child

PRINCE OF CUPS

Star sign – **Pisces**

A lover on the way

Spiritual, emotional man

Creativity

Psychic development

Drugs

Acting on feelings

Not logical

Idealistic nature

Invitations

Proposals

QUEEN OF CUPS

Star sign – **Scorpio**

Maternal woman

Fond of animals

Intuitive, psychic

A home-maker

Attractive, sensual, romantic

Quiet disposition, nervous

Kind and caring

Artistic and creative

Sympathetic friend

Emotional, tears

Not very assertive

Manipulative and possessive

KING OF CUPS

Star sign – **Cancer**

Intuitive man

Dangerous enemy

Highly sexed and emotional

Moody

Jealous nature

Artistic and creative

New age interests

Possessive

Escapist

Heavy drinker

Good counsellor

Warm-hearted

THE SUIT OF PENTACLES REPRESENTS:

Improvements in finances and status

Security

Productivity

Money management, financial advice

Loans, investments, property

Progress, success and recognition

Losses and legal affairs

Hard work

Comforts, materialism

Family

Education

Practical support

Promotions, exam success

ACE OF PENTACLES

Improvement in finances

Good news about money

Good foundations for success

Degree or award

Security within a relationship

Energy directed towards material gain

New businesses, enterprises

Money becoming available

Bonuses, windfalls, gifts

Prosperity and productivity

TWO OF PENTACLES

Juggling with money

Fluctuating income

Restlessness at home/work

Duality in affairs

Becoming more flexible

A casual relationship

Coping with two situations

Dividing of money

THREE OF PENTACLES

Property – buying, extending, improving

Business success

Talent and skill

Progress in work

Recognition or award, exams

Activities within an organisation

Working hard at a relationship

Initial stage in life completed

Ready for hard work to reach goal

Becoming established

FOUR OF PENTACLES

Financial security

Investments

Improvements in work

Comfort at home

Social climber

Miserly tendencies

Afraid of change

Restrictions

Over-protectiveness

FIVE OF PENTACLES

Loss and loneliness

Affairs without love

Financial loss

Settlements

On verge of accomplishment

Neglected health

Loss of faith

Hardship

Temporary setbacks

Unemployment

Solution lies in the rest of the spread

Past extravagance

SIX OF PENTACLES

Gifts of money, legacies

Charity and practical help

Awards, cash prizes

Fortunate circumstances

Faith in oneself and others

Support and sharing

Gifts of love

Give and take in relationships

Promotion

Bonuses

SEVEN OF PENTACLES

Taking a financial risk

Stick to tried and tested or risk a new direction

Negotiating money, loans etc

Slow financial growth

Perseverance

Changes within a relationship

Tiring time, working hard for little reward at the moment

Unpaid work, hobbies, charities

EIGHT OF PENTACLES

Learning new skills

Training and study

Careful financial management

Preparations for a secure future

Personal growth and development

Starting a family

Dedicated to personal goals

New job or promotion

Raise in finances

Skills learned will be relevant to a future career

NINE OF PENTACLES

Buying for the home

Material pleasures

Personal achievement

Relying on oneself

Confidence

Permanence in affairs

Enjoying the fruits of one's labour

Appreciating past efforts

Self-indulgence but well deserved

Love of nature, growing things

TEN OF PENTACLES

Financial matters or family (backed up by court cards)

Inheritance (look for legal cards)

Money, success, material comfort

Unearned money, lump sums

Tax rebates and profits

Practical help from the family

Social family occasions

Family influences

Financial assistance

Heirlooms

Continuing generations – children

Security in all affairs

PAGE OF PENTACLES

A good natured young person

News about money/property

Small financial gain

A steady individual

Good news about family or friends

Warning against theft

Unexpected bills

Skills and talents can be brought to fruition with effort and time

A practical minded person

Junior in a business

Small beginnings from firm foundations

Routine work

PRINCE OF PENTACLES

Star sign – **Virgo**

Loyal friend or business partner

Determination and ambition

Working hard towards a goal

Savings, loans, investments

A cautious young man

News about money/business

Restless person

Faithful lover, very secure

QUEEN OF PENTACLES

Star sign – **Taurus**

Fond of luxury

Interested in history

Practical support

Good organiser/manager

Doesn't like poverty

Tolerant

Materialism

Need for treats and rewards

Selfish with money

Needs a financially stable partner

Kind and warm-hearted

A woman who moves at her own pace

KING OF PENTACLES

Star sign – **Capricorn**

Determined person

Interested in material gain

Excels in organisation

Ambitious man

Works hard for success

Wealthy

Banks, investments

Property owner

Solid, steady, reliable

Financial improvement

Promotion

Conventional person

Miserly with money

Cautious

WHAT THE NUMBERS SYMBOLISE:

ACES (Magician)
  Births and beginnings
  New projects
  Inspiration
  Initiative

TWOS (High Priestess)
  Balance and harmony
  Nurturing
  Union
  Duality
  Relationships between two things

THREES (Empress)
  Growth and success
  Fertility
  Teamwork
  Enterprises
  Creation
  New directions
  Completion of first stage

FOURS (Emperor)
  Structure and foundation
  Logic
  Authority
  Stability
  Temporary restrictions

FIVES (Hierophant)
- Be free from restrictions
- Difficulties
- Pain and sadness
- Battle to be fought
- Fighting against convention
- Anarchy
- Not conforming to rules
- Loss
- Changing attitudes
- Uncertainties

SIXES (Lovers)
- Love, harmony, beauty
- Underlying tensions
- Temporary situations
- Choices
- Finalising settlements
- Moving forward
- Progress
- Rewards

SEVENS (Chariot)
- Inner journeys
- Thinking and meditation
- Seven year cycles
- Progress and change
- Success and rewards
- Hard work
- Warning against excessive pride
- Cautious moves
- Patience
- Morality
- Change and movement

EIGHTS (Strength and Justice)
Structures and foundations
Balancing material and spiritual values
Progress and movement
Clarity
Karma and destiny
Power
Growth and restriction
Expansion
Moving forward
Progression
Stability

NINES (Hermit)
End of a cycle
Positive re-assessment
Self-satisfaction
Attainment
Love
Prosperity

TENS (Wheel of Fortune)
Changes and shifts in life
Fate
Destiny
Karma
Complete happiness
Conclusions
Groups and communities
Beginnings and endings

CARDS FOR DIFFERENT SITUATIONS:

FRESH STARTS/NEW BEGINNINGS
Fool
Death
Tower
All Aces
All Pages

CHANGES AND OPPORTUNITIES
Fool
Magician
Wheel of Fortune
Death
Tower (forced change)
Star
Sun
World
Aces
Pages
Three of Wands
Three of Pentacles
Eight of Pentacles
Ten of Swords

CHOICES AND DECISIONS
Lovers
Justice
Hermit
Hanged Man
Judgement
Two of Wands
Three of Swords (necessary)
Seven of Cups

Seven of Pentacles (risky)
Knight of Swords

CREATIVITY

Magician
Empress
Star
Sun
World
Ace of Wands
Ace of Cups
Page of Wands
Page of Cups
Three of Wands
Queen of Wands
Queen of Cups
Queen of Swords
Prince of Cups
King of Cups

STUDY

High Priestess
Hierophant
Chariot (exams)
Strength
Justice
Hermit
Star
Three of Pentacles
Eight of Pentacles
Page of Pentacles

LOSS
Death
Tower
Three of Swords
Five of Swords (embarrassment)
Nine of Swords (bereavement)
Five of Cups
Eight of Cups
Five of Pentacles

DECEIT, GOSSIP, LIES
High Priestess (secrets)
Tower
Moon
Three of Swords
Five of Swords
Seven of Swords
Ten of Swords
Page of Swords
Queen of Swords
Five of Cups

LOVE AFFAIRS
Two of Pentacles
Lovers
Devil
Tower
Moon
Five of Swords
Seven of Swords
Ten of Swords
Five of Cups
Five of Pentacles
Prince of Wands
Queen of Wands

MOVING HOUSE
Fool
Empress (countryside)
Chariot
Wheel of Fortune
Two of Wands (contracts)
Four of Wands (buying)
Page of Wands
Prince of Wands
Ace of Pentacles
Three of Pentacles
Four of Pentacles

DECORATING
Three of Pentacles
Four of Wands
Nine of Pentacles

LEGAL AFFAIRS
Justice
Judgement
Ace of Wands
Two of Wands
Six of Wands
Ace of Swords
Two of Swords
Three of Swords
Queen of Swords
King of Swords

LOVE, SEX, MARRIAGE
Ace of Cups
Lovers
Page of Cups
Prince of Cups
Two of Cups
Three of Cups (wedding)
Hierophant (wedding)
Devil (sex)
King of Cups (possessive)
Ace of Wands (energetic sex)

FAMILY
Empress (mother)
Emperor (father)
Pages (children)
World (starting a family)
Ten of Swords (upset)
Ten of Cups (permanence)
Ten of Pentacles (support/cash)
Page of Pentacles (good news)

PROMOTION/SUCCESS
Magician
Emperor
Chariot
Justice
Wheel of Fortune
Strength
Star
Judgement
World
Ace of Wands
Three of Wands
Four of Wands

Three of Cups
Nine of Cups
Ten of Cups
Ace of Pentacles
Three of Pentacles
Six of Pentacles

ILLNESS
Strength (recovery)
Death
Tower
Star (recovery)
Nine of Wands (recovery)
Ten of Wands (stress/overdoing things)
Three of Swords (operation)
Four of Swords (recuperation)
Six of Swords (peace)
Nine of Swords
Five of Pentacles (neglected health)
King of Swords (doctor)

LETTERS, NEWS, INVITES
Justice (legal)
Wheel of Fortune
Sun (invite)
Judgement (legal)
Ace of Wands
Two of Wands
Three of Wands
Six of Wands
Eight of Wands
All Pages
All Knights
Three of Cups
Nine of Cups
Ten of Pentacles

FIGHTS, ARGUEMENTS
Chariot
Justice
Strength
Five of Wands (adrenalin)
Seven of Wands (rivalry)

ADVICE
Hierophant
Queen of Wands
King of Wands

HOLIDAYS, BREAKS
Four of Wands
Six of Swords
Eight of Wands (abroad)
Sun

THE END

35875648R00057

Printed in Great Britain
by Amazon